**W9-BYH-177**

Please return to:
**Bates Middle School
Library**
Annapolis, MD

# I Am Israeli: The Children of Israel

## VOICES FROM ISRAEL

Eva L. Weiss

## Mitchell Lane
PUBLISHERS
P.O. Box 196
Hockessin, Delaware 19707

404-33010829   I am Israeli : the children of

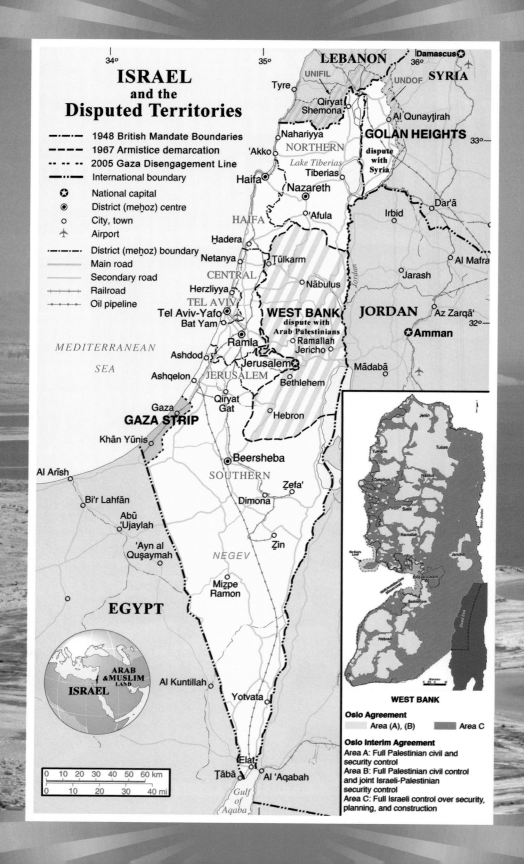

**Mitchell Lane**

PUBLISHERS

Copyright © 2016 by Mitchell Lane Publishers, Inc. All rights reserved. No part of this book may be reproduced without written permission from the publisher. Printed and bound in the United States of America.

Printing     1     2     3     4     5     6     7     8     9

**Library of Congress Cataloging-in-Publication Data**
Weiss, Eva L., author.
I am Israeli : the children of Israel / by Eva L. Weiss.
    pages cm. — (Voices from Israel)
Includes bibliographical references and index.
  ISBN 978-1-61228-685-3 (library bound)
1.  Israel—Juvenile literature.  I. Title.
DS126.5.W465 2015
956.94—dc23

                                    2015010803


**eBook ISBN:** 978-1-61228-694-5

**DEDICATION:** Dedicated to the memory of my father and in honor of my mother.

**ABOUT THE COVER:** Yakir (left), Moshe Me'ori (center), and friend at the Boussidan gallery in Tzur Haddasah. Photo by Zura Bazeli.

**PUBLISHER'S NOTE:** This story is based on the author's extensive research and knowledge of Israel, which she believes to be accurate. Documentation of such research is contained on pp. 59–60.
    The Internet sites referenced herein were active as of the publication date. Due to the fleeting nature of some web sites, we cannot guarantee they will all be active when you are reading this book.

**PRONUNCIATION NOTE:** The author has included pronunciations for many of the Hebrew words in this book. In these pronunciations, the letters "ch" are not pronounced like the "ch" in "children." Instead, the letters "ch" represent the Hebrew letter chet, which sounds like a "kh" or hard "h" sound, similar to the "ch" in "Loch Ness Monster."

PBP

# CONTENTS

**BOLD words in the text can be found in the glossary.**

# Introduction

**M**y name is Yakir (yah-KEER). I am almost eight years old and I live in Jerusalem, Israel. If you spin a globe, it won't be easy to find the country where I live. Israel is smaller than your thumbnail on most world maps. But I feel like I live in the center of the universe.

Everyone's home is unique, and my city and country are special to me. I know my home is a teeny, tiny dot if you think about the earth and the whole gigantic solar system. But it really can't be that small, since we have to make room for more

Yakir

than three million people from all over the world who come to visit Israel during just one year.[1]

I can understand why Israel has so many visitors. My country is an interesting place—and especially fun for children. I am glad my mother decided to write this book about Israel. My friends and I can't wait to tell you why we think it is so interesting to be Israeli. We hope that after you read this book, you might decide you'd like to come here and see for yourself.

**Jerusalem's Yemin Moshe neighborhood**

Nechemia's interests include sports, music, and reading—
especially stories told in comics.

# Introducing Nechemia

**D**ID YOU ASK, "WHAT'S COOKING?"
That's a good question. Many people are under the mistaken impression that if you live in a small town, there isn't much going on. That's not necessarily true. I live in Alon Shvut (uh-LAWN SHVOOT). There are just over three thousand people in my town,[1] but I am busy almost all of the time.

My name is Nechemia (neh-CHEM-yah), and I am nine years old. I have one brother and three sisters. When I am not in school, I like to play basketball, baseball, and also soccer. Soccer is probably the most popular sport in Israel, followed by basketball. But there are children and grownups who play baseball here, too. There is even a little league in Efrat (eh-FRAT), a nearby town, and I am hoping to try out. I am also learning to play the piano from my teacher, who lives down the block and gives me lessons every week. I can play a number of classical pieces, which I like a lot. I also like Israeli music.

If you happen to stop by my house when my Uncle Gil is visiting us, you might find me and one of my sisters in the kitchen. Uncle Gil is a food historian and a chef, and he has taught us a lot about cooking and baking.

Uncle Gil

Significant snowfalls, and scenes like this one, are rare in Israel's Judean Hills.

In December 2013, there was a major snowstorm here in Alon Shvut. It hardly ever snows in Israel, except in the Golan Heights. In that northern region, Mount Hermon is covered with snow during the winter. There is even a ski resort on the mountain. When it snows further south than the Golan Heights, the snow usually falls in Jerusalem and the Judean Hills, the region where I live. But this time, there was also snow in other parts of the Middle East, from Egypt to Syria. Our **prime minister** called it the storm of the century.[2] We are not used to so much snow and it took a very long time to clear the roads. I was home from school for an entire week!

On one snow day, my Uncle Gil came by and we spent the day making cookies filled with nuts and dates. We stayed warm in the kitchen, and our whole family loved the **aroma**. But eating the cookies was the best part! Uncle Gil explained that the recipe for the cookies we made, which are called *ma'amoul* (mah-MOOL), is one of the most ancient pastry recipes still being baked today. That is part of the fun of baking and cooking with Uncle Gil. He teaches us about the history of food and desserts from all over the world.

There are many ways to learn, but my friends and I love the adventures and history we read about in comic books. We think they are very cool. One of my favorite comic books is about a boy who escapes the **Holocaust** and manages to reach Israel.

In the past, immigrants to Israel reached its shores by sea, like the refugees photographed on the deck of this ship in 1948. In our time, new arrivals are welcomed at Israel's Ben-Gurion International Airport.

## Middle Eastern Filled Cookies–Ma'amoul

Baking cookies can give you the chance to prepare a yummy snack and also enjoy the taste of another culture. Nechemia's uncle, food historian and chef Gil Marks, is pleased to share his recipe for ma'amoul, which means "filled" in Arabic. It is one of the most ancient pastry recipes still baked today. Ma'amoul cookies are much loved throughout the Middle East and North Africa. They are served on festive occasions, whether Jewish, Muslim, or Christian. But there is no need to wait for a holiday in order to try these cookies. Gil notes that like most Middle Eastern pastries, the basic dough is not sweet. The filling is usually made of dates or nuts—this recipe uses walnuts, almonds, or pistachios in the filling. Follow these instructions and you will make about 36 cookies.

Before you get started, **remember that it is important to work with a grownup when you bake.**

### PASTRY
3¼ cups bleached all-purpose flour, sifted (or 2 cups flour and 1 cup fine semolina)
2 tablespoons sugar
pinch of salt
1 cup (2 sticks) unsalted butter or margarine, chilled
1 tablespoon orange blossom water or rose water (You can find this at a Middle Eastern grocery store, or a health food or gourmet grocery store)
about 3 tablespoons water

### NUT FILLING
8 ounces walnuts, almonds, or pistachios, finely chopped (about 2 cups)
½ to ¾ cup sugar
1 to 2 tablespoons rose water or orange blossom water
½ teaspoon ground cinnamon (optional)

About ¼ cup confectioner's sugar for dusting

## MAKING THE COOKIES

1. Combine the flour, sugar, and salt. **Cut in** the butter or margarine until it resembles coarse crumbs. Stir in the orange blossom water and add enough plain water to hold the mixture together. **Knead** briefly to form a soft dough. Cover and refrigerate for about 30 minutes.

2. Preheat the oven to 350 degrees Fahrenheit. Line several baking sheets with lightly oiled parchment paper or aluminum foil.

3. To make the filling, combine all the filling ingredients.

4. Form the dough into 1¼-inch balls. Hollow out the balls using your thumb and fill with a heaping teaspoon of the filling. Press the sides of the opening together to cover the filling and gently re-form into balls or crescents. If desired, **score** designs in the dough with a fork or knife. Place the cookies 1 inch apart on the prepared baking sheets.

5. Bake until lightly colored, but not browned—about 20 minutes.

6. Let the cookies stand until firm, about 5 minutes, then transfer to a cooling rack and let cool completely. They become more firm as they cool. Sprinkle with confectioner's sugar. Store in an airtight container at room temperature for up to one week.

Nechemia and his sister Penina

Many boys and girls my age are the great-grandchildren of people who struggled against all odds to get to Israel. So it is important for us to know the stories of relatives, friends, and neighbors who lived just a few generations before us. In school, we learn about the history of the Jewish people and the State of Israel. And just about every Israeli school has a "roots" project. In this program, children interview their parents and relatives and write about their family histories. The children in our class have their roots in many different countries, like Poland, Russia, the United States, Canada, Morocco, Iraq, Iran, Yemen, and Ethiopia.

In my school we learn math, science, Hebrew, and English (but not from comic books). We also study the Bible, the Mishna (MEESH-nah), and the Talmud (tal-MOOD). The Mishna and Talmud tell the stories of the conversations among ancient Jewish **sages** about our heritage and the laws of religion and everyday life.

Ethiopian Jews at prayer in Gondar, Ethiopia. For centuries, the community dreamed of returning to Israel. Today, nearly all Ethiopian Jews live in Israel.

My two favorite classes are the ones in which we talk about our lives at school and outside of school. One class is called Life Skills. In this class, we talk about what we do when we need to solve a problem at school or at home. In another class, called Keys to the Heart, we discuss all kinds of experiences and our feelings about them. I like talking about things that really happened to me and listening to other children's stories.

I am looking forward to our next family vacation. My parents will drive us to Israel's south, which is called the Negev (NEG-ev). We will visit the *Makhtesh Ramon* (MACH-tesh RAM-on) in the Ramon Nature Reserve. Many people mistakenly call it the Ramon Crater, but it is not a crater that was created by a meteor or a volcano. It is a valley surrounded by steep walls that were created by the erosion of the rock that once filled them. Makhtesh Ramon is 450 meters (that is, more than 1,470 feet) deep.[3] There are fossils and rock formations that date back 220 million years.[4] There are also guides who explain the special sights and help us to explore them. And best of all, when we visit Makhtesh Ramon we stay at a hotel with a big swimming pool.

**Ramon Nature Reserve**

## Examining Snowflakes

No two snowflakes are alike, and children who live in Israel's Golan Heights, or any part of the world where there are snowy winters, can learn more about snowflakes by doing this experiment.

You will need a black piece of paper, a camera, a thermometer, and a weather vane. Cover the paper (with a plastic bag, for example) and bring it outdoors during a snowstorm. Wait for the paper to cool, so that the snowflakes won't melt when they land on it. Then remove the cover and catch snowflakes on the black paper. Take a close-up picture of the flakes, and make a note of the temperature and wind direction when the flakes were caught.

Repeat the process at different times during the storm, or even during different storms—but make sure that conditions (such as the temperature) are not the same each time you do it.

The purpose of the experiment is to determine whether the shapes of the snowflakes are different when temperatures and wind conditions change. You can identify your snowflakes by comparing them to illustrations of various types of snowflakes. Dr. Barry Lynn (see next page) suggests that you consult "A Guide to Snowflakes" at: http://www.its.caltech.edu/~atomic/snowcrystals/class/class.htm

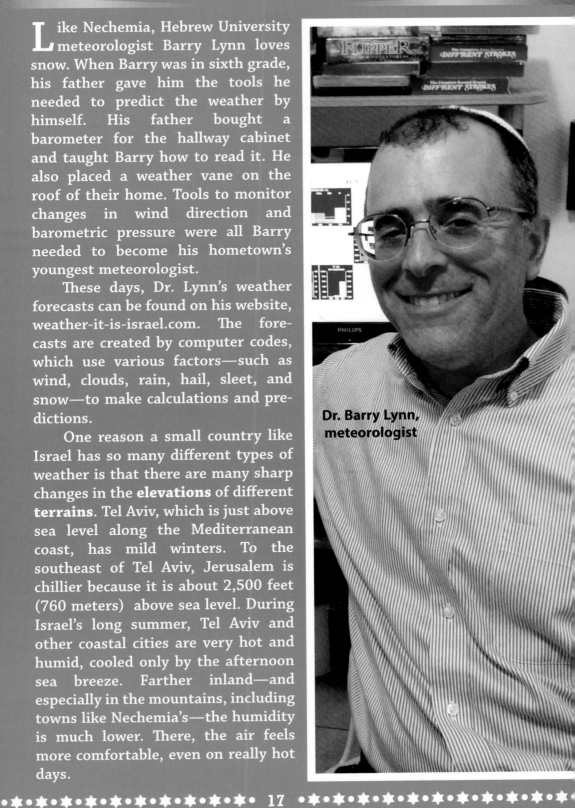

Dr. Barry Lynn, meteorologist

Like Nechemia, Hebrew University meteorologist Barry Lynn loves snow. When Barry was in sixth grade, his father gave him the tools he needed to predict the weather by himself. His father bought a barometer for the hallway cabinet and taught Barry how to read it. He also placed a weather vane on the roof of their home. Tools to monitor changes in wind direction and barometric pressure were all Barry needed to become his hometown's youngest meteorologist.

These days, Dr. Lynn's weather forecasts can be found on his website, weather-it-is-israel.com. The forecasts are created by computer codes, which use various factors—such as wind, clouds, rain, hail, sleet, and snow—to make calculations and predictions.

One reason a small country like Israel has so many different types of weather is that there are many sharp changes in the **elevations** of different **terrains**. Tel Aviv, which is just above sea level along the Mediterranean coast, has mild winters. To the southeast of Tel Aviv, Jerusalem is chillier because it is about 2,500 feet (760 meters) above sea level. During Israel's long summer, Tel Aviv and other coastal cities are very hot and humid, cooled only by the afternoon sea breeze. Farther inland—and especially in the mountains, including towns like Nechemia's—the humidity is much lower. There, the air feels more comfortable, even on really hot days.

Qais near the pool where he swims weekly.

# CHAPTER 2
# I Am Qais

**A**ND **I** LOVE TO MAKE WAVES.
Swimming is my favorite activity and I feel very much at home in the water. There are many places to swim in Israel, from the Mediterranean Sea to the Sea of Galilee (GAL-uh-lee) and the Jordan River. Another possibility is to float in the salty waters of the Dead Sea, which is the lowest shore on Earth. I have been to the Red Sea in Eilat (ey-LAHT), a city at Israel's southern tip, next door to Egypt.

When my family goes on vacation to Eilat, we are always very happy to see the beautiful Red Sea when we arrive. By the way, the Red Sea isn't actually red. It is a clear, bright blue. No one knows for sure how the Red Sea got its name. In ancient languages, directions were represented by colors. Black was north, red was south, east was green, and west was white. It is possible that the sea was described with the word "red" because it was to the south of the ancient Mediterranean world.

The sun shines in Eilat an average of 360 days a year. That is one reason why so many people enjoy taking a vacation there. People visit Eilat from other parts of Israel, and from all over the world. In the summer, the temperature usually reaches 104 degrees Fahrenheit (40 degrees Celsius), so swimming and diving are very popular. In Eilat, or wherever I swim, I prefer a covered pool so the hot sun doesn't burn my skin.

My parents named me Qais (KAHY-yees) for the hero of a famous romantic poem in Arabic literature. The story of Qais

There are many ways to have fun in Israel's seas, rivers, and lakes. The coral reef at Eilat's Red Sea can seem like an underwater garden with its many fish and sea creatures. The Sea of Galilee offers boat rides, and the Dead Sea provides a very relaxing way to float.

Boat on the Sea of Galilee

The Dead Sea

Eilat's coral reef

and Layla is like the story of Romeo and Juliet. My mother imagines that one day I will search for my Layla and that our story will have a happy ending.

In our family, we are convinced that when we work very hard we can make our dreams come true. I believe anything is possible. I walk with the help of **Canadian crutches**, but when I swim, I dart through the water as fast as a fish. I am almost thirteen years old, and since I started swimming three years ago, I have won four medals in competitions. I have a younger brother, Faris (FAH-rees), who is ten, and he is also a good swimmer. We have two younger sisters, but they are both babies, so we don't yet know if they will like swimming as much as we do.

My family lives in Beit Hanina (BEYT hah-NEE-nuh), a Palestinian neighborhood on the eastern side of Jerusalem. We are Muslims and we speak Arabic. The six people in our family are among the 242 million people throughout the world who speak Arabic.[1] Of course, my two younger sisters don't really speak all that much, at least not yet, since they are still very small. But my parents, my brother, and I speak to them in Arabic. They hear our language in the neighborhood, and when they visit our relatives and friends in other parts of Israel.

We study in Arabic in my school, but I also know Hebrew. That's because when I was younger I went to Hebrew-speaking preschools for four years. Even though Arabic is one of Israel's official languages, not many Hebrew speakers know it all that well.

When Hebrew speakers want to learn Arabic, the first phrase I teach them is *"Kaif halak?"* (KEEF HAL-ak) That means, "How are you?"

The answer to that question is *"Alhamdulillah,"* which has five syllables—al-ham-doo-LIH-lah. The emphasis is on the fourth syllable. It means, "Thank God." Of course, that is not really a complete answer, because you are not saying whether you are feeling great, or not so good. It is a way to say that you trust everything will be okay, because there is a good force that guides this world. Hebrew speakers say, "*Baruch Hashem*," (bah-ROOCH ha-SHEM) which means "Bless God," and the meaning is very similar. Not everyone is religious here, but faith and tradition are natural in the language and the culture in this part of the world.

The Muslim calendar has two official holidays, *Eid al-Fitr* (EED al-FIT-er) and *Eid al-Adha* (EED al-AHD-huh). Our calendar also has twelve months, but since it is a **lunar** calendar, the holidays are in different seasons each year. Eid al-Fitr celebrates the conclusion of the month of *Ramadan* (RAM-uh-dahn), a

**Muslim families at a beach in Tel Aviv during Eid al-Fitr.**

time of prayer and reflection. During that month, religious Muslim adults **fast** every day from dawn until sunset. Eid al-Adha is the Feast of the **Sacrifice**, and it celebrates Abraham's willingness to sacrifice his first-born son. Of course, God does not allow Abraham to carry through the sacrifice, so we also celebrate that we are given second chances in life. On this holiday, animals are sacrificed and we share the meat with the poor.

I love both holidays. Our whole family gets together to visit our grandparents. I enjoy the festive meals and all of the good times I have together with my cousins.

Muslim houses of worship, or mosques (MOSKS), have towers that are used to call the faithful to prayer five times a day. This mosque is located in Jaffa, on Israel's Mediterranean coast.

# SWIMMING

Qais shares his love of swimming with his instructor Susan, who has participated in master swim competitions and a charity swim across the Sea of Galilee. This body of water is actually a freshwater lake, and it is known as the *Kinneret* (KEEN-ner-ret) in Hebrew. Susan notes that when you swim in Israel's waters, every stroke takes you through Biblical history.

Swimming and water sports are naturally popular in Israel, a country with a warm climate, many miles of Mediterranean coast, and the shores of the Sea of Galilee and the Red Sea. Because of the freedom it offers, swimming is especially thrilling for people who depend on crutches, wheelchairs, and walkers to move around.

In 1997, Susan studied with Lior Birkan (lee-OR BAR-kon), an Israeli champion swimmer who is also an **occupational therapist**. Susan learned about **hydrotherapy** for disabled people, which was a new field then. Susan discovered that swimming strokes can be adapted to the abilities of the student. Even children who can't lift their heads to breathe in the water can learn to flip onto their backs. For children with **muscular dystrophy**, regular swimming can keep the lungs healthy longer. It can even delay the need to use a ventilator, a machine that helps to move air in and out of the lungs.

There are international Olympic Games for physically disabled athletes, called the Paralympic Games. They were first held in Rome, Italy, in 1960. Many Israelis participate along with other international athletes. Champions are an inspiration, but swimmers of all abilities may also choose to compete only with themselves.

Qais with his
swim instructor, Susan

Gabi enjoys special occasions with family and friends.

# CHAPTER 3
# Go, Gabi, Go!

**I** **AM ELEVEN YEARS OLD AND I AM ON THE RUN!**
I ran in the Jerusalem **Marathon**, along with my sisters, two friends, and about twenty-five thousand others. Both children and grownups ran in the marathon. The other runners included people from across the country and visitors from overseas. There are many marathons, bike rides, and walks in Israel, from the Galilee to the Dead Sea and all the way to Israel's southernmost city of Eilat. But I think the Jerusalem Marathon is especially exciting because as you run, you pass many landmarks. These places tell the stories of three thousand years of Jerusalem's history. You can see ancient Biblical sites; the walls of the Old City of Jerusalem, which were built when the city was part of the Ottoman Empire; and the nineteenth-century train station, which is close to my house.

The historic train station was the first stop on the route that traveled between Jerusalem and the port city of Jaffa (JAF-uh). Before it was built, it took ten hours for travelers to make their way between the two cities by camel or donkey-drawn carts. After the station was opened in September 1892, it took only three hours to travel by train from Jaffa to Jerusalem.[1] Although that train line has been replaced by another route, the site of the original Jerusalem train station was recently restored. The tracks were made into a cool **promenade** that leads across the southern part of the city. I ran along that path many times to practice for the marathon.

On the Friday morning of the marathon, I arrived at the start line, which was near the Knesset (KNESS-et), Israel's **parliament**. I couldn't help but think of "passing GO." I guess that is because my favorite game is Monopoly. Just a few days

Runners along the route of the Jerusalem Marathon.

**A view of Jerusalem's Old City Walls**

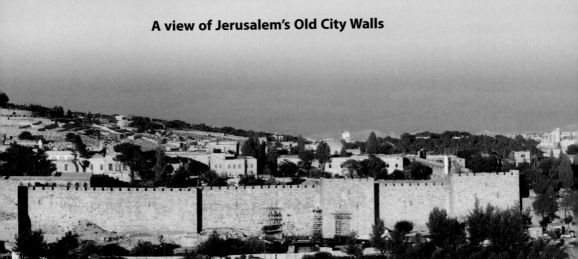

before the marathon, we celebrated the Jewish holiday of Purim (POOR-im), when everybody dresses up in costumes. It didn't surprise anyone that I chose to be Mr. Monopoly, and no one in town had a costume like mine.

There is a Hebrew version of Monopoly, but I like to play with the American version. My favorite properties are the green ones. I like the color green and those properties also happen to have the second-highest rents.

Both of my parents were born in the United States, and so were my sisters and brothers. My parents named me Gabriella, in memory of a relative my family loved very much. But as long as I can remember, my family and friends have called me Gabi. I am the youngest of the five children in my family, and the only one born in Israel. My siblings were worried that I would be different from them, more Israeli than American. But I think I am turning out to be both, and I actually like speaking English even more than Hebrew.

Gabi (center) and her siblings

Gabi (left) and her sisters
at the Jerusalem marathon

Gabi as Mr. Monopoly

When I am not running or playing Monopoly, I have to go to school, which is six days a week, from Sunday to Friday. In Israel, our schedule follows the Hebrew calendar, and Sunday is a school day and a work day. Every culture has its own rhythm, and in Israel our way of life follows the Hebrew calendar.

In Israel, Tuesdays are short school days. That gives us time to participate in youth movements, if we choose. I belong to a youth movement called Ezra. Before I started to attend activities at Ezra, I wasn't sure I would like it. But now I am glad that my friend encouraged me to join, because it is really fun. Sometimes it is a good idea to try something new. Of course, it makes the most sense to take advice from a person you trust. It is important to use your own good judgment. My parents would like it if I asked them for their opinion, too, but I like to think for myself.

Ezra, like most other youth movements in Israel, was established in Europe at the beginning of the twentieth century. At that time, youth movements enabled children and youth to participate in activities that would help them prepare to live in the Land of Israel. Youth movement activities included learning Hebrew, songs and dances of Israel, and how to farm. In those days, many people hoped to become farmers. The youth movements still exist, many years after the State of Israel was established in 1948. In many ways, today's Israeli youth movements are similar to boy scouts and girl scouts in the United States and other countries throughout the world.

Other activities I like are horseback riding, tennis, swimming, and hip-hop dance. I take dance lessons and have performed with my group.

I've visited many places in Israel, including the Negev Desert. It just so happens that my middle name is Sahara, which is also the name of the world's hottest desert. But in an ancient

Hikes and overnight trips to nature reserves are among the activities of Israel's youth movements. The largest of the youth movements is known as Israel Scouts, and the scouts photographed here are on the way to a holiday outing.

language called Aramaic (ar-uh-MEY-ik), my middle name means crescent, or moon. Aramaic is related to modern Hebrew. It is also the language of the Talmud. My father loves to study the Talmud. We share our own opinions when we discuss the sages whose ideas influence Jewish thought to this day.

Negev Desert at sunset

# ISRAEL'S CALENDAR

*W*hat's today's date? That question could be answered two ways in Israel. Israel follows the Gregorian calendar used by most of the world, but its holidays are based on the ancient Hebrew calendar. Hebrew months are either 29 or 30 days, in keeping with the 29½-day lunar cycle. Years generally have twelve months, but every few years, there is a thirteenth month. It is similar to the Gregorian leap year, in which February has an extra day. That thirteenth month, also near winter's end, allows the Hebrew calendar to remain in sync with the 12.4-month solar cycle.

Israelis celebrate the Hebrew new year, *Rosh Hashanah* (ROHSH hah-SHAH-nuh), on the first two days of the autumn month of *Tishrei* (TEESH-rey). The New Year marks the creation of the world, but in Jewish tradition, there are several new years. The fifteenth of the month of *Shvat* (SHVAHT) is the new year for trees, celebrated with tree plantings. And *Nissan* (NEE-sahn) is a new year because it is the month of Passover, the birth of the Jewish nation.

Israel's calendar also celebrates modern milestones. On Independence Day, there are spring nature hikes and barbecues. Holocaust Remembrance Day and the Memorial Day for Israel's Fallen Soldiers are also in the spring. Those **somber** days are observed with a siren and a moment of silence throughout the country. In Israel, most months have a holiday or two, and sometimes three. Each season comes to life with its own festive or reflective mood.

**Soldiers at Mount Herzl, Israel's national military cemetery.**

Yakir always looks forward to his tennis lessons.

# CHAPTER 4
# My Name is Yakir

"**L**ook! Up in the Sky!" Did you know that five hundred million birds fly over Israel each year?[1] I love to watch birds soar through the sky. Sometimes it makes me wish I could fly too. But it is also fun to watch birds from the ground. When I was five, my mother and I drove to the Agamon Hula (AG-uh-mon HOO-la) Ornithology (bird watching) and Nature Park in northern Israel. This park is in between two mountain ranges, the Golan Heights and the Naftali Mountains. You can travel along the nature reserve trail on a bicycle, in a golf cart, or in a safari wagon and observe all kinds of birds as they take flight and land. Some birds spend the entire winter in the Hula Valley and others nest there during the spring and summer. When we were there in the fall, we saw cranes on their way from Russia to Africa and pelicans from the Danube River in Romania.

Over five hundred species of birds fly across Israel,[2] which is a crossroads for three continents—Africa, Asia, and Europe. Although scientists have their ideas, no one knows exactly how all those birds—large, small, and different colors—figure out their flight paths across the world, over land and sea, to make their way to the same places season after season. I wonder if they have a GPS chip in their brains, since they never seem to get lost.

There are over two hundred species of birds that live here in Israel year-round,[3] just like I do. In our science class, we

Migrating cranes in Israel

learned that Israel selected the hoopoe (HOO-poo) bird to represent our country in 2008. In Hebrew, the hoopoe is called *dukhifat* (DOO-chee-foht). I was only two years old when the vote for the national bird was held. The hoopoe bird is brown like cinnamon, with white and black stripes on its wings and tail. It has a tall crest on its head that looks like a crown. Its chirp makes an "oop, oop, oop" sound, which is how it got the name hoopoe.

My name is Yakir Shlomo (shloh-MOH) and I am almost eight years old. Even though I have two names, most people just call me Yakir. I was named in memory of my great-grandfather, and many of my cousins were also given the same name. In Hebrew, Yakir means precious, or dear friend. My second name honors the memory of Shlomo, a special relative of ours. My two names put together mean "dear friend of Shlomo."

Shlomo is Hebrew for Solomon. In the Bible, King Solomon is described as the wisest man who ever lived,[4] and according to tradition, he also knew how to speak the languages of all of

Hoopoe

## Pine Cones Are for the Birds

Birds often fly away just when you would like for them to stay so you can take a closer look. In many countries, making the birds a bird seed and peanut butter snack is a good way to have them stick around for a longer visit on your porch or in your backyard. One way to feed them is to create a bird feeder from a big, open pine cone.

**YOU WILL NEED**
a big, open pine cone
piece of string
peanut butter or vegetable
    shortening
bird seeds
newspaper or paper plate

**INSTRUCTIONS**
1. Find a pine cone you like and bring it home. Work over a paper plate or newspaper to keep your workspace clean.
2. Tie a piece of string to the top of the cone, so you can hang it later.
3. Smear the peanut butter or vegetable shortening on the pine cone's scales.
4. Next you will add bird seeds. You can do this by pouring the seeds into a bowl or plate and rolling the cone around in it so that the seeds stick. You could also sprinkle the seeds on the cone by hand.
5. When you're all done, hang your feeder from a tree and enjoy watching the birds that come to eat from it!

If you live in Israel, the birds may not come to eat from your pine cone. At the Jerusalem Bird Observatory, the guides say that birds in Israel do not seem to like peanut butter or shortening. But since it is so much fun to make a pine cone bird feeder, the Jerusalem Bird Observatory invites children to have fun by painting the scales of pine cones in many different colors. After the paint dries, the pine cones can be tied with rope or string. You can even tie a few pine cones to each other. They are a nice decoration outside or even indoors.

Bird observatory at the Agamon Hula Ornithology and Nature Park

A bird's eye view of the Biblical city of Shiloh

the animals. When I go to the zoo, I like to listen carefully to the sounds the animals make. I sometimes try to speak to them, each in his own language. My favorite animals are elephants and kangaroos.

I also love to play tennis. Last summer, my mother and I walked by a tennis court in my neighborhood and I saw children getting ready to begin their lesson. I liked the shape and feel of the racket and the sound the ball made as it hit against the ground. It turned out that one child was absent that day, and the instructor Ephraim (EFF-rahy-eem) invited me to join.

After that first lesson, I knew I wanted to play all the time. I play twice a week and there is so much to learn: how to hold the racket; the forehand and backhand strokes; and best of all, how to make the ball spin. Ephraim tells us that in order to be good tennis players, we need to carefully plan our moves before we hit the ball. And most important, after the game is over, we must remember to be good sports. That is not always easy, because it can be hard to lose. But no one wins all the time and Ephraim reminds us to enjoy and learn from every game. That is why good tennis players shake hands when the game is over.

After tennis, I am very hungry. My favorite foods are pizza and pasta, which my friends also love. My mother thinks there must be a secret international children's **convention** where we decide on favorite foods. I tell her there is no need for secret conventions. Everyone knows that pizza and pasta are delicious, even grownups. But if there were a secret convention, I would tell children from other countries that they should add *kubbeh* (KOO-beh) to the list. Many families in my neighborhood know how to make this tangy soup with balls made out of **semolina** and stuffed with meat. My neighbor Sonia learned the recipe from her mother, who was born in Kurdistan. We are lucky to have neighbors who are great cooks—and love to share.

Yakir and his tennis
instructor, Ephraim

## Kubbeh Soup the Way They Made It in Kurdistan

Yakir's neighbor Sonia learned how to make kubbeh soup from her mother, who was born in Turkish Kurdistan. She immigrated to Israel with her husband when she was a young mother of six children. Six more children were born to the family in Israel, and Sonia is the eleventh of the brothers and sisters. They made their home right beside Jerusalem's colorful and bustling marketplace, called *Mahane Yehuda* (MAH-chah-ney yeh-HOO-dah). Sonia learned many skills and life lessons from her mother, including a favorite saying: "When the stomach is full, the brain can work."

Yakir couldn't agree more. He is happy when Sonia allows him to help prepare kubbeh soup, the signature dish of families who journeyed to Israel from varied regions of Kurdistan. The word kubbeh means ball or dome, for the round meat dumpling served in a soup that can be flavored with beets or greens. Sonia favors the beet soup, her family tradition. Like her mother, Sonia prepares kubbeh soup over the course of several days: first the meat filling, then the dough, and finally the soup. The dish is central to the family's Friday night meal. The soup is the simplest component of the recipe, and it can be enjoyed by itself, for those curious to taste a time-honored dish. Kubbeh has come to be a comfort food for Israelis with roots all over the globe. **Remember to always work with an adult when you cook.**

### THE DOUGH
6 cups of sifted semolina
1 teaspoon of salt
water as needed

### THE FILLING
1 pound of ground meat (such as beef or lamb)
2 large eggs
1 tablespoon salt
½ teaspoon black pepper
½ teaspoon sweet paprika (available at some gourmet
    or natural food stores)
½ teaspoon cumin
water as needed

## The Soup

1 cup quartered red beets
1 cup diced celery
1 onion, sliced lengthwise
a dash of lemon juice
salt and black pepper to taste
2 tablespoons canola oil
1.5 quarts water
mint leaves to taste

## Instructions

1. Mix the semolina and salt in a large bowl. Add water and mix. Continue adding water and mixing until a dough forms. If you add too much water, you can add more semolina. Cover with a damp towel and set aside for at least 15 minutes.
2. Mix all the ingredients for the meat filling. If the filling is too dry, add water as needed. Set aside.
3. Place all of the soup ingredients in a large pot and bring it all to a boil. Reduce heat and simmer for approximately 30 minutes.
4. While your soup is simmering, break off a ball of dough (about 1.5 inches) and flatten it with your hand. Place some of the ground meat filling onto your flattened dough and press the dough closed, so it completely covers the meat. Make sure there are no holes in the dough (you can add more dough if you need to). Repeat until all the dough and meat is used.
5. Place your kubbeh balls in the soup and cook the soup and kubbeh balls for another 30 minutes.

Sonia and Yakir

Yakir and his good friend Yair (yah-EER) enjoy exploring their neighborhood together.

# TENNIS

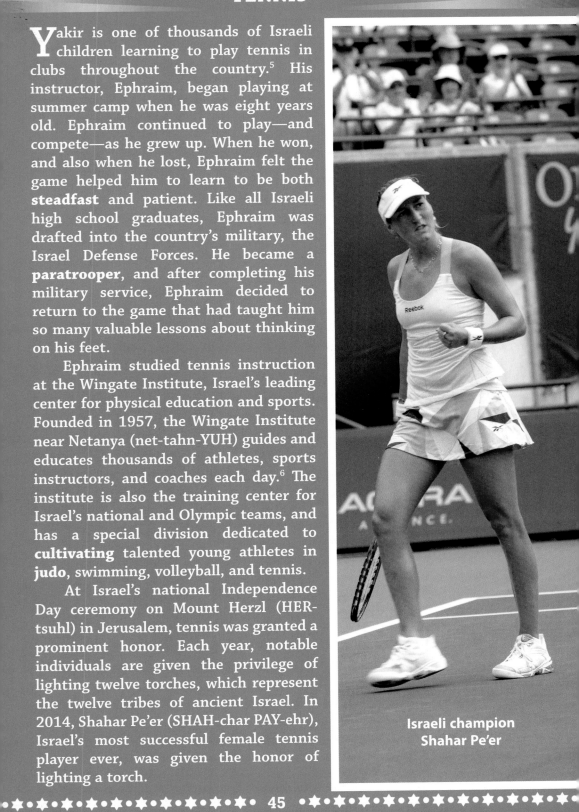

**Y**akir is one of thousands of Israeli children learning to play tennis in clubs throughout the country.[5] His instructor, Ephraim, began playing at summer camp when he was eight years old. Ephraim continued to play—and compete—as he grew up. When he won, and also when he lost, Ephraim felt the game helped him to learn to be both **steadfast** and patient. Like all Israeli high school graduates, Ephraim was drafted into the country's military, the Israel Defense Forces. He became a **paratrooper**, and after completing his military service, Ephraim decided to return to the game that had taught him so many valuable lessons about thinking on his feet.

Ephraim studied tennis instruction at the Wingate Institute, Israel's leading center for physical education and sports. Founded in 1957, the Wingate Institute near Netanya (net-tahn-YUH) guides and educates thousands of athletes, sports instructors, and coaches each day.[6] The institute is also the training center for Israel's national and Olympic teams, and has a special division dedicated to **cultivating** talented young athletes in **judo**, swimming, volleyball, and tennis.

At Israel's national Independence Day ceremony on Mount Herzl (HER-tsuhl) in Jerusalem, tennis was granted a prominent honor. Each year, notable individuals are given the privilege of lighting twelve torches, which represent the twelve tribes of ancient Israel. In 2014, Shahar Pe'er (SHAH-char PAY-ehr), Israel's most successful female tennis player ever, was given the honor of lighting a torch.

Israeli champion
Shahar Pe'er

Moshe Me'ori stands in front of his father's sculpture, called *My Dove, in the Clefts of the Rock.*

# CHAPTER 5
# Meet Moshe Me'ori

**I** **LIVE IN A VILLAGE IN ISRAEL'S JUDEAN HILLS.**
I have two names. The first, Moshe (moh-SHEH), is the name of one of my grandfathers and the second is a name my parents created just for me. They put together the first initials of special friends and family members to form the word Me'ori (meh-OHR-ee), which also means "my light." Everyone calls me by both names, which can sound like one name because you say them together. My two names have five syllables altogether, but they are not so hard to pronounce, even if you don't know Hebrew. You just need to practice a bit.

If you were to come visit me, the first thing you would notice when you enter the gate to our village is a sculpture of two big, white doves. My father tells me that in other parts of the world, such as Europe and North America, buildings—and sometimes even ships—have weather vanes on their roofs or masts. Weather vanes turn in the wind and show you the direction the wind is blowing. My dad says the two doves at the entrance to our village are similar to a weather vane. He calls them the compass to our hearts. One dove faces Jerusalem and the other faces our village. For my family and our neighbors, these are the two places closest to our hearts.

My father is an artist, and he built this sculpture, which he named *My Dove, in the **Clefts** of the Rock*. Those words are from the Song of Songs, a book in the Bible.[1] My dad let me see the sketches he made when he first thought of the idea.

Moshe Me'ori's father, artist Ya'akov Boussidan, at work in his studio.

I was also with my parents when a huge red crane lowered the doves into place on the platform my father designed. It was very exciting to watch my father's idea being brought to life for everyone to see.

I also like to sculpt, paint, and draw. My ideas come to me at night, in my dreams. My dad told me that his mother was an artist, too. She died before I was born, but my dad said that her ideas came to her in her dreams, just like mine do. After I wake up, I remember the images from my sleep. Then I use pencils, paints, and clay to show other people what I imagined in the night, all by myself, in bed. It makes me happy when my parents and my friends like my pictures and sculptures.

Sometimes I draw and paint at home, at my very own table. I also draw and paint at kindergarten, where our teacher tells

**Moshe Me'ori
in his
father's studio**

us stories. Some stories are from picture books, but others are from the Bible, which we call the Torah (TOH-ruh). On Fridays, our teacher also tells us a story from the portion of the Torah that is read in our village **synagogue** on Saturday morning—Shabbat (shah-BAHT). Shabbat is the day of rest, which begins on Friday evening at sunset, and ends on Saturday night. The Torah portion we read on Shabbat changes each week, but the same portion is read in synagogues throughout Israel and all over the world.

In my kindergarten, and in kindergartens throughout Israel, we prepare for Shabbat on Friday morning. Soon after we arrive, we roll, braid, and bake a yummy Sabbath bread called *hallah* (CHAH-luh). Our teacher places our hallah rolls in the oven, and they are ready in time for the ceremony to welcome Shabbat, just before our parents come to take us home. For the ceremony, two children, a girl and a boy, are chosen to be the *Ima shel Shabbat* (EE-mah shel shah-BAHT), the Sabbath Mother, and the *Abba shel Shabbat* (AH-buh shel shah-BAHT), the Sabbath Father. Everyone gets a turn. The Ima shel Shabbat

Torah scroll

Sabbath candles, wine goblet, and braided hallah

puts a scarf over her head and blesses the Sabbath candles, which she lights together with the teacher. The Abba shel Shabbat recites a prayer called *Kiddush* (kee-DOOSH). We all drink grape juice and eat hallah. On Friday, our day at kindergarten ends at noon. We go home early to give everyone enough time to prepare for Shabbat.

I love our Friday night dinners at home and every so often we have guests who stay with us for all of Shabbat. We know the Sabbath is over when we can see three stars in the sky on Saturday evening. Sometimes, just as the sky begins to darken, my parents and I like to take a walk to visit my father's sculpture. We stand on the platform next to the two doves and together we search for three bright stars in the deep blue sky. By then, it is almost time for me to go to sleep. I look up into the night sky and wonder what I will dream.

# Date Balls

One of Israel's most popular homemade children's desserts is chocolate balls, or *kadoorei shokolad* (kah-DOHR-ay SHOOW-kah-laht) in Hebrew. Children, parents, and preschool teachers often prepare chocolate balls as a birthday or school activity, covering them with coconut and candy sprinkles. Moshe Me'ori's mother, Ruth, enjoys date balls instead. They are also great fun to roll and eat. And dates are mentioned in the Bible as one of the seven species of fruits and grains that make the Land of Israel special (along with wheat, barley, grapes, figs, pomegranates, and olives).[2]

There are nine varieties of dates grown in Israel. You can use the variety of date you like best (dates are grown in many countries throughout the world, including the United States). Ruth recommends you use vacuum-packed dates, pitted of course. They are the easiest to crush in a food processor. You can also add crushed nuts. Moshe Me'ori's friend Yakir likes to add a few spoonfuls of sesame seed paste, known as *tehina* (teh-HEE-nuh) in Hebrew. After you combine and process all of the ingredients and roll the paste into a ball, you can roll them in coconut slivers or cocoa powder—or both.

Before you get started, **remember that everything done in the kitchen, especially with food equipment, should be done with a grownup for safety**.

### INGREDIENTS
2 cups pitted dates, from a vacuum-packed package
2 tablespoons sesame seed paste (optional)
1 cup dried almond slivers
3-5 tablespoons cocoa powder
3-5 tablespoons shredded coconut

### INSTRUCTIONS
1. Place the dates, almond slivers, and sesame seed paste in a blender or food processor, and blend well.
2. Shape the mixture into balls
3. Roll them in the cocoa powder or the coconut slivers. You can also roll them in both.

4. Depending on the size of the balls, you should have 15 to 20 balls. Place them in the refrigerator for two hours before serving. Extras can be stored in the freezer, in the unlikely event that any are left over.

## Create Your Own Artist's Book

Moshe Me'ori's father, Ya'akov Boussidan (YAH-ah-kohv BOO-see-dahn) explains what an artist's book is in the sidebar on page 56. If you would like to create your own artist's book, Ya'akov suggests you begin with a story that is close to your heart. It can be a tale written in a book, a poem you love, or even a message that you find scrawled across a wall. You choose the text, and you choose how to interpret it. You can write on paper, cloth, poster board, paper bags, or any material that you would like to stitch together to make a book. Let your imagination soar, and use pencils, paints, clay, buttons, or even scraps to form letters and images to bring your artist's book to life.

Here is one plan to put your artist's book together:

Gabriela Hannah

### MATERIALS
scissors
brown paper bags, cut into rectangles,
    approximately 10 x 15 inches
several pieces of white or colored
    8.5 x 11-inch paper, cut in halves,
    for the pages
poster board, cut into two
    5.5 x 8.5-inch rectangles,
    for the covers
stapler
glue
paint and paintbrush, markers, colored pencils, cloth, buttons, scraps,
    glue, or anything else you'd like to use to create your images

### INSTRUCTIONS
1. Decide on a story or poem, and plan the number of pages your book will need. Calculate how many paper bag rectangles you will need to make the number of pages you want. One paper bag rectangle will give you two pages, plus a back and front cover. Each additional rectangle will give you four pages. So if you would like to have a ten-page book, you will need three rectangles.
2. Stack your paper bag rectangles neatly, and fold them in half to create the base of your book. About ½ inch from the fold, staple the "spine" of your book a few times.

3. Create your images and words on your paper halves. These pages will later be glued onto your paper bag pages, so you can place them in the book to see how they will appear. You can also cut extra halves if you would like to practice your designs before you make your final pages. Remember to keep your pages in order once they are complete so you know where they belong in your book.

4. Create your cover designs on your poster board rectangles. If you are using paint or glue, let everything dry before moving on to the next step.

5. Put just a bit of glue on the back of a finished poster board or paper page. Be careful not to use too much glue, or you might smear your designs or glue your pages together. Place your designs where you would like them to be in your book. You may want to place a piece of paper over your book, and then place a heavier book on top of it to hold everything in place while it dries.

The instructions above are just one way to build an artist's book. You don't have to limit your ideas to paper, paints, and pencils. Use any materials you choose.

Yakir's cousin Gabriela Hannah visited Ya'akov's studio in Tzur Haddasah (tzoor ha-DAH-sah). When she saw Ya'akov's Haggadah, it reminded her of the Haggadah she and her classmates had made when they were in second grade. Instead of drawing or painting a Haggadah, the class used Lego blocks to build scenes from the Passover story. They built people and objects that told the story of slavery and freedom that they had studied. They then took photographs of their Lego scenes and used the pictures to create the art for their book. Together with the words of the Passover story, their Haggadah was complete. Gabriela remembers that she and her classmates couldn't have been prouder.

**Using Lego blocks to tell the Passover story**

# WHAT IS AN
# ARTIST'S BOOK?

**M**oshe Me'ori's father, Ya'akov Boussidan, is a sculptor, painter, and printermaker. He explains that in an artist's book, the artist **interprets** the text of a book that he or she loves through the colors, forms, and materials of his or her imagination. The words of the book or poem provide the inspiration. Ya'akov spends days, months, and even years thinking about how to **transform** words into art.

The Haggadah (hah-gah-DAH) is a book that describes the rituals of Passover and tells the story of the ancient Hebrew people's escape from slavery in Egypt. Ya'akov worked for eight years on his Haggadah and recalls it fondly as a labor of love. He wrote the classical text of the Haggadah in his own original **calligraphy**. Each letter in Ya'akov's Haggadah was written to reflect the beauty of the Hebrew alphabet and the art in the world around him.

Ya'akov created his Haggadah with the assistance of thirty students. They helped him grind and mix the raw materials that would become the paint for his book. They also helped him to make the paper and the heavy zinc plates that were used to print a limited edition of sixty copies of the Haggadah. It is the first Haggadah known to be fully etched in color and it is part of the permanent collection of the Israel Museum in Jerusalem. It can also be found in the New York Public Library and private collections around the world.

**A traditional folk song in Ya'akov Boussidan's Haggadah.**

# CHAPTER NOTES

## Introduction
1. Central Bureau of Statistics, "Visitor Arrivals in Israel," January 2015, http://www1.cbs.gov.il/hodaot2015n/28_15_030t1.pdf

## Chapter 1: Introducing Nechemia
### DID YOU ASK, "WHAT'S COOKING?"
1. Central Bureau of Statistics, "Israeli Settlements, 2013," [Hebrew], http://www.cbs.gov.il/ishuvim/ishuv2013/bycode.xls

2. *Times of Israel*, "Netanyahu Says Disaster Averted in 'Once-in-a-Century' Storm," December 14, 2013, http://www.timesofisrael.com/netanyahu-says-disaster-averted-in-once-in-a-century-storm/

3. UNESCO World Heritage Centre, "Makhteshim Country," http://whc.unesco.org/en/tentativelists/1486/

4. Yaakov Skolnik, "Makhtesh Ramon Nature Reserve," trans. Brenda Malkiel and Miriam Feinberg Vamosh, Israel Nature and Parks Authority, 2002, http://www.parks.org.il/ParksAndReserves/ramon/Documents/ramonEn.pdf

## Chapter 2: I Am Qais
### AND I LOVE TO MAKE WAVES
1. M. Paul Lewis, Gary F. Simons, and Charles D. Fennig, eds., "Summary by Language Size," *Ethnologue: Languages of the World, Eighteenth edition* (Dallas, TX: SIL International, 2015), http://www.ethnologue.com/statistics/size

## Chapter 3: Go, Gabi, Go!
### I AM ELEVEN YEARS OLD AND I AM ON THE RUN!
1. The First Station, "The History of the First Station," http://www.firststation.co.il/en/category/history

# CHAPTER NOTES

**Chapter 4: My Name is Yakir**
**"Look! Up in the sky!"**

1. The Israel Ornithological Center, http://www.birds.org.il/en/bird-center-page.aspx?centerId=10

2. Israel Ministry of Tourism, "Israel Paradise for Birds," 2011, http://goisrael.com/Tourism_Eng/Articles/Attractions/Pages/Israel%20paradise%20for%20birds.aspx

3. Tomer Landsberger, Avner Cohen, and Eyal Vanunu, "Birds of Israel—Checklist," Israbirding.com, The Israeli Birding Website, http://www.israbirding.com/checklist/

4. 1 Kings 5:9-11, in Harold Fisch, English editor, *The Holy Scriptures* (Jerusalem: Koren Publishers, 1992), p. 408.

5. Richard Weber, "Israel Tennis Centers Closes Out 2014 with Special Olympics Competition," Israel Tennis Centers, Globe Newswire, January 14, 2015, http://globenewswire.com/news-release/2015/01/14/697455/10115587/en/Israel-Tennis-Centers-Closes-Out-2014-with-Special-Olympics-Competition.html

6. Wingate Institute, "Basic Information," http://www.wingate.org.il/Index.asp?CategoryID=478&ArticleID=661

**Chapter 5: Meet Moshe Me'ori**
**I Live in a Village in Israel's Judean Hills**

1. Song of Songs 2:14, in Harold Fisch, English editor, *The Holy Scriptures* (Jerusalem: Koren Publishers, 1992), p. 857.

2. Deuteronomy 8:7-8, in Harold Fisch, English editor, *The Holy Scriptures* (Jerusalem: Koren Publishers, 1992), p. 221.

# WORKS CONSULTED

Boussidan, Ruth (graphic designer and mother of Moshe Me'ori). Interview with the author, February 24, 2014.

Boussidan, Ya'akov (artist and father of Moshe Me'ori). Interview with the author, February 24, 2014.

Boussidan, Ya'akov. *Jerusalem: Names in Praise*. Jerusalem: Keter Press Enterprises, 2005.

Central Bureau of Statistics. "Israeli Settlements, 2013." [Hebrew] http://www.cbs.gov.il/ishuvim/ishuv2013/bycode.xls

Central Bureau of Statistics. "Visitor Arrivals in Israel." January 2015. http://www1.cbs.gov.il/hodaot2015n/28_15_030t1.pdf

Eban, Abba. *Heritage: Civilization and the Jews*. New York: Summit Books, 1984.

Ephraim (Yakir's tennis instructor). Interview with the author, March 25, 2014.

The First Station. "The History of the First Station." http://www.firststation.co.il/en/category/history

Fisch, Harold, English editor. *The Holy Scriptures*. Jerusalem: Koren Publishers, 1992.

Gabi (age 11). Interview with the author, February 28, 2014.

Gabriela Hannah (age 11, Yakir's cousin). Interview with the author, February 16, 2015.

Israel Ministry of Tourism. "Israel Paradise for Birds." 2011. http://goisrael.com/Tourism_Eng/Articles/Attractions/Pages/Israel%20paradise%20for%20birds.aspx

The Israel Ornithological Center. http://www.birds.org.il/en/bird-center-page.aspx?centerId=10

Landsberger, Tomer, Avner Cohen, and Eyal Vanunu. "Birds of Israel—Checklist." Israbirding.com, The Israeli Birding Website. http://www.israbirding.com/checklist/

Lewis, M. Paul, Gary F. Simons, and Charles D. Fennig, eds. "Summary by Language Size." *Ethnologue: Languages of the World*, Eighteenth edition. Dallas, TX: SIL International, 2015. http://www.ethnologue.com/statistics/size

Lynn, Barry (senior lecturer, the Hebrew University of Jerusalem). Interview with the author, March 30, 2014.

Marks, Gil (culinary historian and chef). Interview with the author, April 21, 2014.

Marks, Gil. *Encyclopedia of Jewish Food*. Hoboken, NJ: John Wiley and Sons, 2010.

Moshe Me'ori (age 5). Interview with the author, February 24, 2014.

Nechemia (age 9). Interview with the author, April 21, 2014.

Qais (age 12). Interview with the author, March 16, 2014.

Skolnik, Yaakov. "Makhtesh Ramon Nature Reserve." Translated by Brenda Malkiel and Miriam Feinberg Vamosh. Israel Nature and Parks Authority, 2002. http://www.parks.org.il/ParksAndReserves/ramon/Documents/ramonEn.pdf

# WORKS CONSULTED

Sonia (Yakir's neighbor). Interview with the author, March 26, 2014.

Susan (special education teacher and Qais's swimming instructor). Interview with the author, March 16, 2014.

UNESCO World Heritage Centre. "Makhteshim Country." http://whc.unesco.org/en/tentativelists/1486/

Weber, Richard. "Israel Tennis Centers Closes Out 2014 with Special Olympics Competition." Israel Tennis Centers, Globe Newswire, January 14, 2015. http://globenewswire.com/news-release/2015/01/14/697455/10115587/en/Israel-Tennis-Centers-Closes-Out-2014-with-Special-Olympics-Competition.html

Wingate Institute. "Basic Information." http://www.wingate.org.il/Index.asp?CategoryID=478&ArticleID=661

Yakir (age 7). Interview with the author, March 24, 2014.

# FURTHER READING

Grossman, David. *Duel*. New York: Bloomsbury Children's Books USA, 2004.

Kaplan, Kathy Walden. *The Dog of Knots*. Reston, VA: MAB Books, 2004.

Podwal, Mark. *Jerusalem Sky: Stars, Crosses, and Crescents*. New York: Bantam Doubleday Dell Books for Young Readers, 2005.

# ON THE INTERNET

Agamon Hula: A Paradise for Birds and People
http://www.agamon-hula.co.il/?lang=en_US

Israel21c: Top 32 Summer Activities for Kids in Israel
http://www.israel21c.org/travel/top-32-summer-activities-for-kids-in-israel/

The Israel Museum, Jerusalem
http://www.english.imjnet.org.il/

Jewish Virtual Library
http://www.jewishvirtuallibrary.org/

Mediatheque: The Mediatheque Theatre for Children and Youth
http://www.holon.muni.il/English/Culture/Pages/Medi.aspx#01

Shoshana Meerkin's watercolor art
http://shoshanameerkin.com

The Society of the Protection of Nature in Israel: Explore Natural Israel
http://natureisrael.org/Explore-Natural-Israel

Ya'akov Boussidan: Haggadat Boussidan
http://boussidan-y.com/wp-content/uploads/haggadah-highlights.pdf

# GLOSSARY

**aroma** (uh-ROH-muh)—a pleasant smell that usually comes from food or plants

**calligraphy** (kuh-LIG-ruh-fee)—decorative, beautiful handwriting

**Canadian crutches** (kuh-NEY-dee-uhn KRUHCH-iz)—crutches that help people who cannot walk on their own; Canadian crutches are fitted just below the elbow, at the forearm, making it easier to climb stairs and use one's hands

**cleft** (KLEFT)—a split or opening

**convention** (kuhn-VEN-shuhn)—a formal meeting to discuss and make decisions on specific topics

**cultivate** (KUHL-tuh-veyt)—to improve or develop by training or teaching

**cut in**—to mix a hard, creamy substance like butter or shortening into a dry powder like flour, in a way that there are still small lumps or crumbs of the cream in the mixture

**elevation** (el-uh-VEY-shuhn)—measurement of the height above sea level of a specific place

**fast**—to stop eating or drinking for a period of time, sometimes as part of a religious holiday

**Holocaust** (HOL-uh-kawst)—Germany's attempt to kill the entire Jewish people and other people during World War II

**hydrotherapy** (hahy-druh-THER-uh-pee)—exercise that is done in water to improve the condition of an injury or illness

**interpret** (in-TUR-prit)—to explain the meaning of

**judo** (JOO-do)—a martial art and combat sport that originated in Japan

**knead** (NEED)—to press, fold, and stretch dough until the texture is the same throughout the dough

**lunar** (LOO-ner)—measured by the cycles of the moon

**marathon** (MAR-uh-thon)—a foot race that is twenty-six miles (forty-two kilometers) long

**muscular dystrophy** (muhs-KYUH-ler DIS-truh-fee)—a disease that weakens the muscles and makes it difficult for affected people to move their bodies fully

# GLOSSARY

**occupational therapist** (ok-yuh-PEY-shuh-nuhl THER-uh-pist)—someone trained to help people who have trouble in carrying out the tasks of daily living

**paratrooper** (PAR-uh-troo-per)—a soldier trained to parachute from an airplane

**parliament** (PAHR-luh-muhnt)—a group of people who are responsible for making laws for their country, or the building in which they meet

**prime minister** (PRAHYM MIN-uh-ster)—the head of the government, usually in a government with a parliament

**promenade** (prom-uh-NAHD)—a public area used for walking

**sacrifice** (SAK-ruh-fahys)—to give up an animal, plant, or human life as a religious act

**sage** (SEYJ)—a wise person

**score** (SKOHR)—to make decorative lines or ridges in dough by pressing the back of a fork or other utensil lightly into the dough

**semolina** (sem-uh-LEE-nuh)—hardened wheat used for preparing pasta, cereal, and other wheat-based foods

**somber** (SOM-ber)—serious and sad

**steadfast** (STED-fast)—committed to a certain direction or purpose, and willing to continue working towards that purpose despite obstacles

**synagogue** (SIN-uh-gog)—a Jewish house of worship

**terrain** (tuh-REYN)—an area of land, especially referring to its specific natural features

**transform** (trans-FAWRM)—to change something from one form into another

**Photo Credits:** Design elements from Thinkstock and Dreamstime/Sharon Beck; Cover, p. 1—Zura Bazeli; p. 2 (map)—Jaakobou/United Nations; pp. 2–3 (background), 3–4, 11, 21 (top), 32, 33, 36, 37, 38—Thinkstock; pp. 6, 7, 28–29 (top)—Noam Chen/Israeli Ministry of Tourism, www.goisrael.com; p. 8—Barbara Mitchell; pp. 9, 15—Debbi Cooper; p. 10—Alexey Kljatov; p. 13—Elli Schorr; p. 14—Dmitri Kessel/Time Life Pictures/Getty Images, (inset)—Eic413/Public Domain; pp. 16, 20–21 (background)—Dafna Tal/Israeli Ministry of Tourism, www.goisrael.com; p. 17—Icrat Miriam Lynn; pp. 18, 25, 34, 41, 43, 44, 64—David Rafailovich; p. 20 (bottom, front), 39—Itamar Grinberg/Israeli Ministry of Tourism, www.goisrael.com; p. 21 (bottom)—Aronbrand/Dreamstime; pp. 23, 24—Dana Friedlander/Israeli Ministry of Tourism, www.goisrael.com; p. 28—Sharon Altshul; pp. 26, 30—Jared Bernstein Photography; p. 32 (top)—Dnahev/Dreamstime; pp. 34, 41—Alan Meerkin; p. 39, 53—Aryeh Wiseglass; p. 45— Zairbek Mansurov/Dreamstime; pp. 46, 56—Ya'akov Boussidan; p. 48—Ruth Boussidan; p. 49—Dr. Aron Portnoy; p. 50—Daniela Weiss; p. 51—Miri Pyle; p. 52—Tomert/Dreamstime; p. 55—Manyakotic/Dreamstime; p. 64 (watercolor painting)—Shoshana Meerkin.

# INDEX

# About the Author

Eva L. Weiss is a writer and editor. She was born in New York City, but has lived for many years in Jerusalem. Eva and her son Yakir enjoy exploring Israel—and the world—by reading books and visiting new places. She wrote this book to introduce young readers to just a few of Israel's remarkable children.

　　Writing a book can be fun, even if it is demanding. For authors of all ages, it is a task that requires patience and fortitude. It may help to keep in mind the words of the artist Vincent Van Gogh, "Poetry surrounds us everywhere, but putting it on paper is, alas, not as easy as looking at it."

Please return to:
**Bates Middle School**
**Library**
Annapolis, MD

| DATE DUE | | | |
|---|---|---|---|
| | | | |
| | | | |
| | | | |
| | | | |
| | | | |
| | | | |
| | | | |
| | | | |
| HIGHSMITH #45114 | | | |